FRAGRANCE OF WORDS

ABEER KHATRI

Contents

Preface

My work is a piece of my hard work of some years. Some of it coming from very personal and overwhelming lived experiences. I want it to get a global and strong presence. I want it to get, the representation my voice and perspectives yearn to deserve.

This is a collection of forty six poems written over a period of time. These are penned based on my lived experiences with each of the titles. The poems are divided into four themes – Life, Relationships, Learning, Abstract and, Emotions.

It will be a great read for general readers, young adults, adults, philosophers, academicians and, good for a short and interesting read. It has conventional and refreshing topics yet it is unconventional in its approach. Moreover, it leaves the reader pondering over the everyday aspects of life. Along with the larger things and issues at play in life. Readers across locations and intersections have something to take from the book.

I am Abeer Khatri. I live in Mumbai, Maharashtra, India. I completed B.A., M.A., M.Phil., in Sociology. Also cleared the state and national level eligibility tests for lectureship in Sociology. And got a national level scholarship for five years for conducting doctoral research in Sociology. I have taught Sociology at the post graduate level for two years. I am currently writing the thesis for my Ph.D.

Writing is my passion. Creative writing interests me the most. I am an avid reader.

I have a knack for details which helps in researching and gathering nuanced information. Sharply and keenly placing these details as per the requirement is also an efficiency I possess. Interesting word play ensures my writing keeps the reader engrossed.

1. LIFE

Childhood

Naturally given to all

Stays for some up to – teenage or young adulthood, well into adulthood

However, the extent and expression can stay forever too

The child within comes out in comfortable presence or the best presence – the self

For some, it vanishes as soon as they are forced by life to take up responsibilities of adulthood in childhood itself

Society

A general group or body of people

Presumably with commonalities and distinctiveness

A closed ghetto of the privileged communities with myriad complexes on either sides of the gate

The killer of many breaches and non-conformism

The ironic keeper of the apparent ideals and harmonies

Patriarchy

Crux of society

Deeply embedded everywhere

Source of privilege to some,

Vulnerability of most

Systems and agents work within its framework,

For a breach would invite sharp ire
Power and control are maintained because of it
Therefore, a strong and persistent movement to dismantle the
patriarchy
Adolescence
A transitionary phase
The state of becoming
Clinging on to the slipping childhood
Reluctant to accept or leave the approaching maturity
Rush of emotions, power play of hormones
Eventful period - puberty, peers, menstruation, career, family,
society, relationships, the self,
All fighting for a pie of this overwhelmed young adult in the
making
The end of this phase, and memories and experiences to last a
lifetime
Adulthood
It is here to stay for many years to come
Everyday life is a stage performance
Many temporary bonds and relations
Few childhood and teenage bonds – strengthen and sustain, some
vanish forever, some become need based
Responsibilities, identity, hobbies, career,
Struggling and juggling through all
Finding solace - looking into the mirror,
At the still surviving childlike spirit within
Age

Just a Number
Suffrage
Lifetime, Century, Years Gone By
Milestones - Infancy, Toddlerhood, Childhood, Adolescence,
Teenage, Young Adulthood, Adulthood, Middle Age, Old Age
All defined by Society although Biological
It is the age lived to the Fullest that Matters
Otherwise it is only Counting the Years

Lock - Unlock

Locked down - the city
Unlocked - cleaner air
Locked - workplaces
Unlocked - work from home
For the woman, the site of double burden became one
Locked - Employment and Income for many
Unlocked - Opportunities to retrospect, reflect, relearn, again
bond for many
Locked in - with the abuser/(s)
Unlocked - the strength to report abuse at last

Life

Life is lived only to die ultimately
When taking the material aspects too seriously
Think of the time when you,
Gave to the soil Your everything (human)
And one day you will give,
Your own self

2. RELATIONSHIPS

Family

Tied by blood, affinal kin

Shelter and nurturer

Complementary and ascribed

A feeling of being with beloved ones

Eating, fighting, living, enjoying, managing as an entity

Friends become family

Some families become friends

Cousins

Family - Living Together or Separately

Related by Blood

However it is the Affinity that Matters

Friends and Foes

Have your Back Always

Or Tear you up with Envy

Your Glimpse of the Supportive Society

Or your Lived Nightmare of the Critical Gaze

Fun and Frolic, Tears and Tragedies,

Lived Together, Sharing and Caring,

Sealing the Bond

Friendship

Choice made by the self

Achieved affinity over time with trust, love, care and support
Not family (by birth) but equally staple
A tree grounded with deepest roots,
Accepting every fruit
This ship sails in the turbulent and calm waters of life, with
equal paddling on both sides

Marriage

Meeting of Two Souls
Union of Two Bodies
Alliance between Two Families
A Social Institution
License to Rape
License to Reproduce
Lifetime of Companionships or Bondage
Patriarchal Sacrament or Contract
Matter of Choice or Force
One or Many in a Life
Basis of Upbringing and Socialisation of many Girls
Of Children and Adults
Common and Equally Complex
Loved and Equally Hated!

3. LEARNING

Education

Basic Necessity and Investment
Privilege for Many
Ideally Egalitarian
Actually can be Discriminatory
Learning the New
Relearning the Forgotten
Unlearning the Flawed
For Degree and Employment
Education for Holistic Development
Vocational and Traditional, Soft Skills and Life Skills
Application is a Task
The need to Reform Education Systems at specific intervals
Also ensuring education for All

School

From a Toddler to a Teenager,
Spending more than a Decade of Life's Formative Years
Agent of Socialisation
Inculcator of Life Skills
Friendships for Life
From the first day to the last day,
All the Memories comeback as Nostalgia, on every visit thereafter

As the Institution is Etched in your heart, mind and soul,
So are you, not only in its Records but also in the Memories and
Hearts of your Educators

College

A Collage of Memories,
Learning, Unlearning, Relearning, Experiences
Teachings for Life,
Friends for Life
Education, Degree(s)
Hangouts, Events, Teamwork,
Trailer for the Film of Life
Campus, Canteen, Class – Buzzing with Dreams, Fun, Efforts
and, Hopes
A Full Circle from – Fresher's Party to Farewell to Alumni Meet

Sociology

Study of the society, for a common person
The continuous and never-ending contestation between the
systems and agents;
The battle of determining who forms whom
The fray within the branches for gaining roots
Myriad perceptions of everything
The loveliness and messiness of getting, keeping and accepting it
all together

Subaltern

The tussle between the mainstream and the periphery;
The popular and the ground reality

The need to maintain control; the aim of being heard and
gaining power
Can be reflected in the struggles of some natural and social
sciences
Or that between allopathy and homoeopathy; quantitative and
qualitative sociology

Research

Searching, looking - again
Understanding, analysing;
Problematizing, critically questioning
Exploring - the topic, the world, the SELF
Processing, Concluding - Assimilating, Theorising, Publishing
Achieving Doctorate
Finding - Everyday, mundane things - ideas, people, services,
products, businesses
Also hunting for Peace and Happiness

Reading

An Addiction, An Aversion
Gateway for a Literary Getaway
Takes you with it to its World
Worded Picture Paints in the Mind, Vivid Imaginations and
Realities
The Power of the Twenty Six Alphabets,
To create Immensely Meaningful Worded Worlds

Writing

Appears easy, is difficult
Looks exciting, is exhausting

The way we talk, the task is to make the written speak
A passionate creativity of making the paper vocal
The mind, heart, soul, come together and make the pen or
keyboard work with hands
Sometimes the tongue laughs due to the ease with which it
communicates
The pen or keyboard then chuckle because they can make many
tongues move the way they want

4. ABSTRACT

Dream(s)

Lets the eyes close as well as open
Makes one lose sleep over it or because of it
Some dream to live and some live the dream
Gives new, meanings, hopes, experiences and the instinct to live
When a dream is lived, it catches the eye more than the dream
catcher catches the eye

Ambitions

Driving force, chief ingredient to keep the stew of life brewing
The salt of the concoction minus which life is tasteless
Elated is a woman when her ambitious grit breaks the stereotypes
society creates for her
Ambitions, the fuel and need to maintain self-esteem and
continue to grow...

Guide

The answer to all queries – a book
The living map for a traveller – a tourist guide
The presence of an experienced supporter – a research supervisor
The go to person in all situations – a best friend
Always prepared – a girl guide
A path shower and explainer – a guide; in many roles dwells this
soul

Struggle

Makes you or breaks you
Perseverance and sustenance help till the end as best friends
Tests are appeared then lessons are learnt
Taxing the strengths,
Weaknesses are recognised
Privileges and vulnerabilities at loggerheads
Result is an achievement and / or an experience

Achievements

Work harder, work smarter
With each win and task complete comes an accolade to the galore
of achieved feats
Material and non-material,
Achievements are here to stay
However, the battle between the ascribed and the achieved status
continues to date

Escape

An attempt to run, to disappear maybe
Met by an attractive and glamourous creation
The cinema
Lived experience, lets get carried away
Living an alternate life for few hours
Fulfilling the need to escape
Walking back to be absorbed into the existing…

Conversations

Beauty of face-to-face conversations
Privilege of virtual video conversations

Fulfilling telephonic conversations
Emotive virtual conversations
Telepathic and eye conversations win the game
The unsaid and that which is left unsaid may haunt for a
lifetime

Expressions

Many forms,
Overt and covert.
Written, typed, verbal, virtual, emotive, behavioural, facial,
artistic, and all
The best of them all is the one expressed and understood as given
Expressing is a task; equally gruelling is its perception, processing
and criticism or acceptance
It is this expression that reveals and conceals, simultaneously

Listener

The valuable and uncommon art of listening
A non-judgemental, empathetic possessor of this art
The listener in a - researcher, friend, therapist, dear one
A purposeful listener, a professional listener, the selfless listener
Listening to the said and the unsaid, the verbal and the
non-verbal
The reliever of burdens, the gatherer of information

Presence

Of mind – tasks smooth
Of heart – feelings soothe
Of listener – burdens cease
Of educator – ignorance sieged

Of family – life's blissful
Of friend – life's delightful
Of dream – continuous efforts
Of achievement – completeness
Of experience – wisdom
Of absence – lesson

Missing

Longing for someone precious
Absence of something important
Missing an everyday affair for some eventually becoming a habit
The best missing is when the hope to meet again rekindles each
moment
The worst missing is the missing of the presence of someone close
yet far away, geographically and emotionally

Soul Sister

May not be related by blood,
However more important than flesh blood
Soul connects with this soulmate,
Such that a reflection of the self in the mirror
Eyes do the conversations,
Telepathic connections
Complete belief keeps grounded and lets them soar heights

Unconditional Love of a (Social) Fat "HER"

Making someone your everything
Giving that someone your everything
Seeing that someone grow through leaps and bounds
Training that someone for things in Life

Nurturing through your everything
Letting that someone be independently
Peacefully watching with pride and glee
Being "she" with glimpses of your reflection
Then ceasing to be
Making her reflect and think the importance and need of the
training, growth, independence and being "her", in myriad
phases of life... ❤?❤?❤?

Moon

Bright, blooming, prominent, enlightened
Smaller, visible, clear
Persistent, illuminated
Present yet invisible
The tidal and gravitational power, effects on humans
The Luna - the representor of the feminine
Both equally powerful and unrecognised
The beauty and evil of the status of subtle powers

Time

Injures, Heals
Takes, Gives
Past, Present, Future
Sun, Moon, Tide, Zone
Day, Night, Season
Clock, Calendar
Happy, Sad
Not the Same Always
Keeps Passing

Phases

Pass or Save

Being with it is the key to Balance

After all, it is ALL ONLY A MATTER OF TIME!

Memories

Good and Bad

Lessons Learnt

Lasting Impressions

A Closet Full of Varied things

Like Chocolate – Milk, Dark, White

Powerful Enough to – Ail and Heal

Some to be Stored, Some Discarded

Photographs and Photographic

Wealth

Health - Physiological and Mental

Valuable and Invaluable Possessions

Plenty, Sufficient, Abundance, Crucial, Need, Indispensable,

Disposable, Redundant

Material, Non Material

Material Gives - Affluence, Power, Comforts, Luxuries, Friends,

Foes

Non Material Gives - Love, Affection, True Buddies, Enemies,

Gratitude, Contentment

Complete Well-Being!

ALL

The emptiness and nothingness of it ALL!

The ever enveloping cape of sadness

The sieved escape routes;
The means of the needed oxygen
The epitome of stuck and blocked
The struggling writer
The doomed creativity
The afloat and lost entity

5. EMOTIONS

A Bond

Love accepts

Breaches begin and continue

Ego rejects

Soul suffers

Heart handles

Mind manages

Hatred creeps in

Body reacts and imbalances

Therapist enters, helps sort out

Love triumphs and prevails

Block/(s)

Many together, a child's play;

An act of creative display

Many houses as a cluster;

The neighbourhood hustle and bustle

A pause of creativity in prose, a stagnation of ideas and thoughts

Lump of grief in the throat, a blot on the soul, the raging ego,

the imbalanced being

Indifference

Differences in differences;

Indifference is different

Lack of understanding
Inability in grasping
Sheer attitude
Temporary relief from, looking at, facing and fighting, living in
the present
A defiance, a feeble manner of keeping an enclosure;
To procrastinate and appear unperturbed

Pride
Of doting parents, friends and dear ones
Self-esteem of a confident personality
Wrenching egotism
Adamant wish of the ego to triumph
Devastating when reaches the head
Buffer between the id and the super ego
Dwells in the reality

Pain
Physiological; bruised, imbalanced, ruptured body
Psychological; hurt mind, crushed feelings, pounding heart
Social; vulnerable agents within privileged systems
Fellow humans; broken bonds, lost lives, devastated achievements

Curtly
The Hurt Heart
The Meddled Mind
The Scarred Soul
Manifested by the Stinging Tongue
Sharply through the Larynx
Emanated Curtly Toned and Placed Alphabets

Thus, a Bruised Being got termed a Rude and Curt Human

Sympathy and Empathy

Sympathy listens and helps soothe,

Common yet temporary,

Easy to find and accept.

Empathy feels, believes, tries to live and understand,

Frugal yet lasting,

When found, helps heal and persist

Gratitude

Deep yet superficial

Easy to assume

Expressing is laborious

An art, to express, understand and accept

Achieved through efforts

Rarely received though important

Gratitude

I am indebted to my aunt for life. Whatever I am in life is only because of her. The flaws being all mine. Her love and everything that she did for me in her life has only led to my growth and development. My deepest gratitude to my mother, who is my polar opposite. However, her love, efforts and support have been my strength. I am thankful to Juveria and Sana for always doting on me and addressing me as their fire brigade. It such unconditional love and friendship that keeps one going. I am indebted to my field of Sociology. It has made the person that I am in myriad ways. It taught me to be holistic, critical and, inclusive in my approach, at the same time acknowledging interdisciplinarity and multiple perspectives. My love for reading and writing only grew and doing sociology has helped it grow leaps and bounds. I am thankful to all my educators, over the years, they not only imparted knowledge to me but also taught me how to see and think rather than what to see and think. Their teachings have been a guiding light for me all through. I am thankful to all the readers who read this book. It is my first publication and hence, holds a special place. Your decision of buying and reading this book, takes me closer to my life goal and passion of being a bestselling author of fiction writing and poetry. Writing this book was like photocopying my mind on paper. That you have reached till the end here, is such a respect to my efforts of putting my perspectives in poetry. There is more following....